Series consultant: Dr Terry Jennings

Designed by Jane Tassie

The author and publishers would like to thank Selvi, Jahmarl
and the staff and pupils of the Charles Dickens J & I School, London,
for their help in making this book. Thanks also to James Parkin.

A CIP record for this book is available from the British Library.

ISBN 0-7136-6327-8

First paperback edition published 2002
First published 1999 by A & C Black Publishers Limited
37 Soho Square, London W1D 3QZ
www.acblack.com

Typeset in 23/28pt Gill Sans Infant and 25/27 pt Soupbone Regular

Printed in Singapore by Tien Wah Press (Pte.) Ltd

A & C Black uses paper produced with elemental chlorine-free pulp,
harvested from managed sustainable forests.

Science Explorers

Metal

Exploring the science
of everyday materials

Nicola Edwards and
Jane Harris

Photographs by
Julian Cornish-Trestrail

A & C Black · London

Metals have lots of different uses. We've collected these metal objects.

Look at all the shapes and sizes.

2

I've found some tiny objects.

3

Metals come
from under
the ground.
Most metals
are found
in rocks,
which are
drilled out
and crushed.

The rocks
are heated
to make the
metal melt.
When the
metal cools,
it turns into
a solid block.

5

There are many different types of metal. Very strong metals are used to make bridges, boats and cranes.

This metal climbing frame is solid and sturdy.

Some metals are light and bendy.

7

This metal saucepan is shiny and heavy. It has smooth surfaces so that it's easy to clean.

I can cut through the paper easily.

It feels cold and hard.

These metal scissors have a sharp edge.

This jumping ghost has a metal spring inside it.

I push the spring down...

...and watch the ghost jump!

Metals can be made into all kinds of shapes.

This flower pot was made in a mould.

The metal is heated, then poured into a mould. As the metal cools down, it sets into the shape of the mould.

My box is made of flat pieces of metal.
They have been bent into shape and
joined together.

The box
is light but
strong.

Metal allows heat to travel through it. Let's find out if heat travels best through wood, plastic or metal.

We've put a wooden spoon, a metal spoon and a plastic spoon in a jug of warm water for two minutes.

Iron and steel are magnetic. This means that a magnet will pull these metals towards it.

We've made a magnetic fishing rod!

We tied a steel magnet on to a piece of string.

We're finding out which of these metal objects are magnetic.

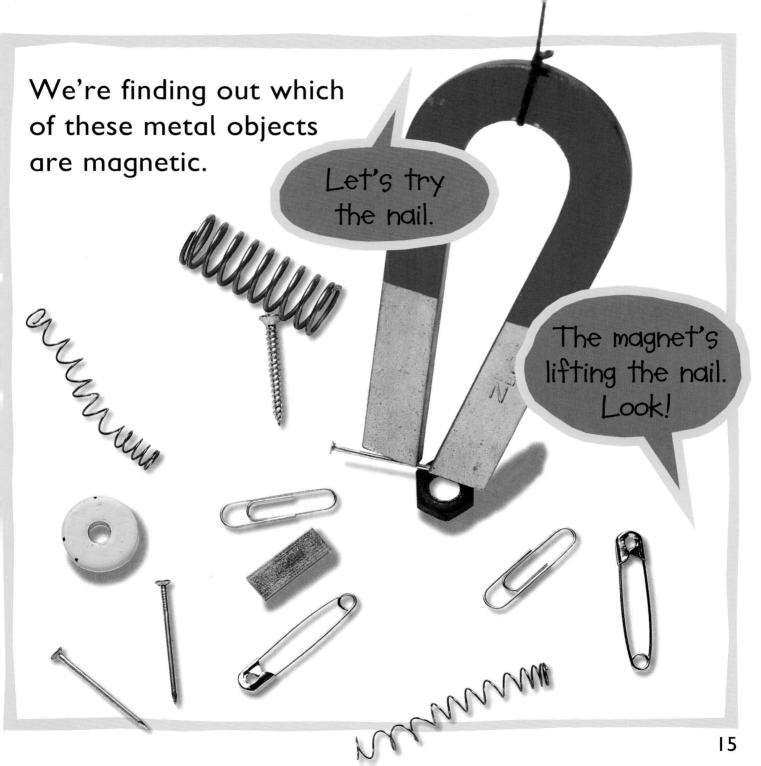

Our cutlery is made of stainless steel. Other metals were added to the steel to stop it from rusting.

This kitchen tool is made of metal. What will happen if I drop it?

It bounces and it makes a noise.

We've been for a walk
around the school to
look for metal objects.
We've made a list.

It's time to tidy away. Many metal objects can be recycled and made into new things.

We've made this recycling box for our school.

We've collected lots of cans to put in the box.

This sign shows that it can be recycled.

23

Notes for parents and teachers

The aim of the *Science Explorers* series is to introduce children to ways of observing and classifying materials, so that they can discover the various properties which make them suitable for a range of uses. By talking about what they already know about materials from their everyday use of different objects, the children will gain confidence in making predictions about how a material will behave in different circumstances. Through their explorations, the children will be able to try out their ideas in a fair test.

pp 2–3

There are more than a hundred known elements, from which everything in the world is made. More than three quarters of these elements are metals. While each metal has certain properties that distinguish it, all metals have a number of things in common. They all reflect light, are shiny in appearance and are good conductors of heat and electricity. All metals are silver or grey in colour apart from copper which is reddish, and gold which is yellow. Metals play a huge part in our everyday lives and they have done so for thousands of years. As early as 3,500 BC, gold was used for making ornaments, jewellery and utensils.

pp 4–5

Only copper, gold, silver and platinum can be found as pure metals. Other metals are found in rocks called ores and are usually combined with other substances. Some metals, including iron and copper, are purified by smelting – the ore is crushed and heated in a furnace so that the hot liquid metal can be extracted.

pp 6–9

Each metal has different properties which makes it useful for particular things. For example, tungsten is used for filaments in light bulbs because it does not melt until heated to 3,400°C. Aluminium is very light and is used to make aircraft, boats and cars. It can also be rolled into very thin sheets and is used to make metal foil and drinks cans. The children could explore the different properties of a variety of metal objects, investigating weight, pliability and magnetism. Are the objects smooth or sharp; are they springy or solid; do they chip or crack if dropped?

pp 10–11

Most metals can only be shaped when they are heated. This is done in different ways, such as casting, rolling or extrusion. Metal pieces can be joined using nuts and bolts or by more permanent methods, including welding, soldering or riveting. Look at some everyday metal objects and discuss how the pieces have been joined together.

pp 12–13

Metals are good conductors of heat; the atoms are tightly packed together so that the vibrations are quickly passed on through the object. As an extension of the test on page 12, provide a variety of utensils that are made of metal but have plastic or wooden handles. Ask the children to predict what will happen when they are placed in the jug. If possible, use a plastic jug (if the children handle glass, ensure that they are properly supervised).

pp 14–15

Iron, nickel and cobalt are the only pure metals that have strong magnetic properties. Children could explore magnetism further using a magnet to manoeuvre paper-clips on a piece of paper.

pp 16–17

Over time, many metals will corrode and weaken. Corrosion occurs due to the chemical action of a gas or liquid on the metal. Rust is the most common form of corrosion and affects objects made from iron or steel when they are exposed to moist air. Stainless steel contains nickel and chromium and resists rusting.

pp 18–19

Most metals are solid and hard at room temperature and will not crack or break if dropped. When a metal object is struck or dropped, it vibrates, causing it to make a sound. Percussion instruments in particular tend to be made of metal. The children could make their own percussion instruments, using metal objects.

pp 20–21

Encourage the children to imagine a world without metals. What substances are there which could replace metals? Did the children know, for example, that keys were once made out of wood?

pp 22–23

Recycling metals saves energy and reduces pollution. Discuss the importance of recycling and, if possible, take the children to a recycling centre that collects metal objects.

Find the page

Here are some of the words and ideas in this book.